MAGGIE CHARDONNAY

Exploring Neuromarketing in Wine

PIERRE SPAHNI

ISBN: 978-1-4834-5320-0 (sc)
ISBN: 978-1-4834-5319-4 (e)

Lulu Publishing Services rev. date: 06/29/2016

PREFACE

The idea for this piece came with the chance discovery of the book *Neuromarketing for Dummies* by Stephen Genko, Andrew Pohlmann and Peter Steidl. Their brilliant work provides the frame and the canvas for our little story, which also focuses on wine attributes, a concept developed in two books I worked on in the early Nineties. It is a subject that I have always held dear and have followed ever since, albeit from a distance. The sources I have used are all grouped thematically at the back.

Maggie Chardonnay is a personification of the 'Chardonnay girl' profile created by the drinks wholesaler Waverley TBS in its segmentation of British wine drinkers in the early Noughties. A more recent, but less sophisticated, attempt at segmenting the Swiss market is used as a backdrop for the novella.

But is this a novella or a little book on wine marketing?

It is a new format and to help wrench my text into it I have had the great pleasure of relying on Neil Wenborn's exceptional qualities as both an editor and a writer. For only one thing was clear from the outset: this 'thing' had to be kept short and sweet.

Thanks too to the local artist Percho for applying her unique talent to the cover. This book is dedicated to the wonderful Geneviève.

I

The tips of her skis seem to glide effortlessly on top of the powder. It's a perfect day. Silence is broken only by a light breeze and the cadence of Maggie's energetic turns. An excellent skier in search of deep virgin snow, she's descending a narrow corridor. She's cut off from the rest of the world and gets this incredible feeling of oneness with her magnificent surroundings.

Suddenly, the whole slope moves down the mountainside, at ever greater speed. She can't really control her skis anymore. Everything seems to slide down with her. "Blast! It's an avalanche," she thinks. She falls. Everything goes white.

Maggie wakes up.

"Gosh, it's Saturday and the shops close at five. I've got to do my shopping for the weekend."

She slips into a pair of jeans and dashes out of the flat.

The household names of the Swiss high street – Coop and Migros, the largest retailers, and Denner the discounter – are all just a stone's throw from her place, and that's quite handy. Maggie needs wine for her meals and heads for Coop's food hall because she's short on time and doesn't want to wait twice at a cash register when she can do it all at once (Migros doesn't sell any intoxicants).

She sets herself in "habitual shopping" mode upon entering the store and walks straight to the dairy corner. "I need milk, a couple of yoghurts, a bit of cheese – just the regular stuff, really." Then on to the ready-meals section. No bread ("it makes you fat and can be bought at petrol stations 7/7"). Items are picked off the shelves automatically, almost briskly, and dumped in haste into her basket (she can't be bothered to take one of those trolleys that slow you down and make you buy more than you need). She finally gets to the wine section and goes for her usual pick: "a bottle of Shiraz and a bottle of Chardonnay will do fine". A nearby bottle of Malbec at a 30% discount catches her eye (she likes it but its normal price falls well outside her regular range of 10–12 francs); it ends up in the basket, which is now getting heavy. Time to head for the nearest checkout.

There she has to wait.

She has too many items for the express lane and would not be tricked into doing self-scanning in order to cut down the processing time at the end of the shopping experience. Two people are standing in front of her.

"How come they make it so easy for you to buy your stuff and when you've got to pay they make you wait?" she asks herself, tapping her fingers impatiently on the basket. "I hate it." She gazes into space for a moment. "But then who likes to wait and who likes to pay?" Maggie surmises that parting company with money is a painful act for everybody – not just her – and that shops try to ease that pain by allowing her to use a plastic card or a smartphone instead of cash. She is also confident that the shop won't let her stand in line for too long and that someone will open another till for fear that she'll defect to the competition.

"I might try Denner next time," she tells herself. "It's fast, they've got all the essentials and a good selection of New World wines."

Maggie loves New World wines because they're easy to choose, easy to open and easy to drink. Cabernet, Chardonnay, Semillon, Shiraz – the taste of the wine is written large on the label and there is often a short description of it on the back label, usually giving a few suggestions for food pairing. She likes the styles of those wines and has never been disappointed by them.

"Brands are like people," she feels: "if you like them, you build expectations; if later they keep failing to meet them, you just move on to others, however difficult dumping them may seem to you."

Strong brands deliver reliable quality. They hardly ever fail. And once you've found your brand you can really trust it and experiment with it. That's what Maggie likes about New World brands.

She's not as comfortable with geographical indications, which could well be thought of as collective brands but are too inconsistent, in her view, to be fully trusted. OK, when buying in a café or in a store where none of her favourite brands are featured she'll default to a Montepulciano d'Abruzzo, a Chianti Classico or some other geographical name, hopefully combined with that of the dominant grape variety, like a Pinot Noir from the Valais, but she'll never pick a Bordeaux ("it's overpriced and *passé*"), except as a gift to someone old and staid.

As for the remaining attributes of a wine (colour, strength, fizziness, packaging and price), it depends on what she's buying it for: to accompany her meals or just to relax, alone or with a few friends, or even to celebrate! She is aware that whenever she picks a wine, she chooses not just a bottle with an attractive label or a nice name on it, but a "bundle of attributes" that will deliver certain benefits (functional, emotional) for the occasion and mood she is in or intends to be in.

Although Maggie senses that she is unwittingly playing into the hands of marketing people who know there are clear links between benefits and attributes and have cleverly framed the little bits of information put at her disposal, she isn't exactly troubled by it. Somehow her grounding in psychology makes her aware of the fact that her perception of wine attributes depends on the context in which they are presented to her and that in following her own emotional guide when choosing a bottle she is taking a few evaluation and decision shortcuts (she would readily admit preferring a discount expressed in percentage terms to an equivalent one shown in francs, for instance). These shortcuts have helped her intuitively assign value to the various offers proposed to her throughout the food hall and they have simplified considerably the choices she has just made. They have turned most of her shopping decisions into implicit ones and as a result her decision process has been largely intuitive and non-conscious.

But has this made her fail to "choose" any of the three bottles of wine now lying in her basket? The Chardonnay and Shiraz could be credited to her habitual shopping pattern, i.e. to opting for the comfort of a familiar brand. She didn't feel like taking the time to look at other bottles on display and run the added risk of being disappointed by them later. So that question didn't cross her mind at all whilst waiting in line at the cash register. She did start to muse on whether the extra bottle of Malbec was all that necessary, however. Did she fall prey to the shop's savvy promotion and buy a 30% reduction that happened to bring the wine closer to her habitual price band?

"Don't really know," she says to herself and begins to rationalise her extra purchase whilst putting her groceries onto the cashier's desk. "The promotion might only have lasted for a few weeks, and maybe Steph will cook some pasta if we decide to end up at my place tonight, and…"

Maggie feels slightly guilty because she knows that whenever she begins to rationalise, there's something fishy about her decision. Years ago, she read in an old book on applied psychology that whenever people start to rationalise they are only finding sensible arguments for what their primal self has already decided subconsciously. Trust, beliefs and taste are all rooted in the primal self, the author claimed, and they have to be infused with information provided by advertising. You can't appeal to consumers' capacity to assess the quality of a product on an objective basis because they don't usually have that capacity. You can appeal to their trust, however, and it is vital that consumers have blind trust in a brand name. The advertisers' job is to provide consumers with a set of (pseudo-)rational arguments so that they are persuaded their choice proceeds from these rational(-like) arguments and not from the publicity itself.

"That's spooky," she says to herself as she realises that marketing people have known these facts and applied them in Europe for well over half a century.

"45.75 please," says the cashier.

Maggie gives her a 50 franc note, together with a smile.

"4.25 change. Have a nice weekend!"

"Thanks. Same to you!"

Maggie dashes back towards home. She's due to meet Steph on the terrace of the Cactus Bleu in just under an hour and she hasn't taken her shower yet. The last images of her dream flash back to her and put her mind in a whirl. She's determined to stay on top of it and stops for a brief moment. She leans against a parked car. Freja's motto springs to her mind: "Just float, take it easy, float through life."

"Quite right," she tells herself and smiles again.

Freja is her favourite fashion model, and there are strong hints of Freja's natural cool in Maggie's character. OK, Maggie isn't quite as tall and her body may not have been graced with the same sort of striking beauty, but she's slender and graceful and her looks rarely go unnoticed, which can be quite handy at times. She is gentle but can also be a bit wild. Later, at home, after stepping out of the shower she goes straight to the mirror, stares into it and pouts.

"Do I still look like a true Chardonnay girl?" she wonders aloud.

Being born in Davis to an eccentric and ravishing Californian mother (the legendary Terry Chardonnay from Woodland, who vanished without a trace in the haze of the San Francisco Bay) might look like excellent credentials, but are these really sufficient?

"Well," she reckons, "if partying's in my DNA, I must surely qualify."

Maggie knows that it only takes a handful of very specific traits to match the profile of the famous British "Chardonnay girl": she goes to modern pubs and wine bars, has lots of big nights out and sociable get-togethers in the city centre, she likes fresh flavours and fruity wines and has a wide drinks repertoire. She hasn't got a lot of money but she's got youth (she's under twenty-four).

So, barring her age – she is thirty-five but young at heart – Maggie feels she has kept the profile of a true "Chardonnay girl". This is in spite of her having spent well over a decade in Geneva, where her father eventually settled. As luck would have it, the austere spirit of the city has not yet managed to dampen her determination to live life to the fullest. To her, glasses are never half-empty; they are always full – preferably of sparkling wine. Perhaps it's that she's still young enough to resist conformity and dullness, or perhaps it's her foreign genes that have provided her with some form of immunity to these afflictions. Be that as it may, her undaunted optimism rests partly on the fact that she has spent too many years immersed in philosophy, psychology and art whilst having serious fun in Edinburgh to think that living in a Calvinistic city necessarily makes you dull, and partly on the fact that she has chosen to live on the edge of the city, close to the more laid-back Carouge, where she's due to meet up with Steph.

II

Eight small fried shrimps ("cocos" in local parlance) are neatly arranged in a bowl in front of her. They are about to be shared with her younger friend Stephanie. Steph is a twenty-year-old hairdresser of Portuguese descent. They plan to go out together later on, but they have still not figured out whether they will go to a gig, or to a movie followed by a pizza, or simply have yet more tapas and wine. Who cares? It's a bright, sunny day and they are both in an excellent mood. They feel just fine.

Maggie grabs a shrimp by the tail and dips it into the red sweet-and-sour sauce.

"Did you know that Carouge was actually built in the same enlightened period as Edinburgh's New Town?" she says. "This ambitious development by the king of Piedmont–Sardinia was meant to compete with the free city of Geneva. And so was Versoix, the French rival version championed by Voltaire. Well, they were both gobbled up by the Swiss in around 1815 – just like a coco…"

"Let us stay for a while and order some drinks," says Steph, who is decidedly unimpressed by the whole Enlightenment thing.

"If only they had sparkling wines from the New World," says Maggie. She settles for a Prosecco.

"A Prosecco?" Steph wonders aloud. "But there are local bubbles on the wine list. There's even Champagne!"

"Champagne is overpriced and the sparkling wines from around here are dull," comes the answer. "Plus they remind me of the countryside. Did you know that there's a place a few miles from here that's called Champagne and the winegrowers can't even use that name? There's a village in the state of Vaud that has the same problem. Those French! I'm glad they sort of left two hundred years ago."

Maggie raises her empty glass in their honour.

Steph orders a guacamole with a Petite Arvine from the Valais.

Maggie considers herself to be a citizen of the world (another enlightened idea). She is genuinely surprised by Steph's loyalty to indigenous wines. "Steph isn't even a Swiss national," she thinks, "so why does she bother to drink Swiss? Granted, she was born in the Valais, one of the best wine-growing regions, but then she spent her late teens around Porto before moving back to Switzerland. Well, I guess she's just one of those *indifférent* wine drinkers who buy mostly from supermarkets and on someone else's recommendation. She's certainly not a Chardonnay girl! Here we are misfits by default, who fall into the broad category of the *curieux* because we couldn't possibly fit into either of the two remaining types of Swiss consumers, the stuffy *traditionalistes* and the wealthy *internationalistes*."

Then, out of the blue, Maggie remembers reading about Spanish researchers who had found that some people associate local wines with higher quality simply because buying them boosts their cultural identity (the awareness of helping local growers gives them a feeling of social belonging).

"So maybe Steph drinks Swiss wines because she needs to feel integrated," Maggie muses, "and if enough people think like her, if enough of them lack curiosity, then Swiss wines have a pretty good time ahead of them. To beat foreign wines in a country full of easily pleased Stephs, domestic producers would only need to boast about their origins on the label. That's crazy," Maggie thinks, but prefers to keep it all to herself for fear of offending Steph.

The waiter brings the two glasses of wine at last, together with a guacamole. It's getting pretty busy. The only remaining free table is a small round one, right next to them.

"*Voilà* your foreign bubbles," says Steph and smiles whilst gently pushing the Prosecco towards Maggie.

Maggie raises her glass to Steph. "A toast to free trade," she says in a slightly defiant tone, smiling back at her. "Look at Carouge," she continues. "I don't just like it because it's pretty – it was designed by neo-classical urban planners from the Piedmont – but because it's the product of the Enlightenment, of people freeing their minds from the burden of tradition."

"What do you mean?"

"Economic liberalism, for one thing. It was still in vogue when Carouge and Geneva joined the Swiss. Local winegrowers benefited from this. It pushed up demand and prices for wine, triggering a wave of investments in new vineyards all around here, many of them highly speculative."

"Really?"

"Yes, and roughly the same happened in the other wine-producing cantons of Valais and Neuchâtel, who joined Switzerland at that time, as well as in the newly fledged state of Vaud. This eventually led to an oversupply of Swiss wines, but freedom always breeds excesses. That's just the way it is. In spite of this, I remain a staunch liberal in all strands of life. Freedom comes at a price."

"But you've read about the strong franc," says Steph. "Surely, domestic wine producers can't be blamed for it, so we've got to help them a bit?"

"Yeah, yeah, they keep moaning about everything. They're very French in that respect, out there in Geneva's countryside. Don't you think they keep turning their back on what feels like a distant Switzerland – like Alain Tanner says in his Seventies film *La Salamandre*?"

Maggie pauses for a second. She's gazing at a biker parking a sleek black Kawasaki near the terrace. "He certainly has taste," she thinks, then adds aloud: "Some even want to go back to the old days when protectionism was the rule and strip me of my beloved Chardonnays from the other side of the world. And you'd be sorry too, because the price of your Petite Arvine would go up and its quality would probably go down over the years – or at least fail to improve as much as it would in the face of serious foreign competition. Domestic producers would be much less keen to innovate."

"How do you know that?"

"It's by raising quality that the Swiss managed to get out of the doldrums a hundred years later, in 1915," says Maggie. "But when the wine market was flooded with French surpluses again and closed to foreign competition, in the early Thirties, some feared that the quality of domestic wines would deteriorate once more."

"So what?"

"Well, history proved them right: white wines became insulated from foreign competition until the market was forced open sixty years later. The reds were subjected to much less severe trade restrictions and they've held up rather well against their foreign competitors. White wines, by contrast, have kept losing out to imports. This can only mean that, over time, protection leads to a drop in quality."

Maggie is satisfied with her demonstration. She swallows a coco before adding: "But then again, what is quality?"

"Come on, Maggie," says Steph, "we're not going to dig into that question now. Even philosophers have gone crazy over this. Remember the guy you talked to me about the other day, who wrote a famous book about Zen and motorcycle maintenance."

"Exactly," replies Maggie, who can't take her eyes off the handsome biker. "Robert Pirsig is his name. He literally went mad when he attempted to find out what quality means. It cannot be defined, he says. To him, 'quality' is identical to 'value', which some find a bit extreme. He wrote another book on it later, called *Lila*, in which he says that quality is a kind of 'sense of betterness', and if you have that sense of betterness then you necessarily resist conformity. You become a bit of a rebel and you're pushed to the margin of society. I quite like that."

"If quality is value, doesn't a higher quality mean higher prices?"

"Not at all. As a hairdresser, you know that you can have quality at every price level. But then again, we know that it pays to sell dear whilst hammering home the message that your product is of higher quality than the others: consumers will ultimately believe that you are telling the truth. The French have applied that strategy successfully to the appellations Bordeaux and Champagne, and many people are still convinced that, because they are more expensive, those wines are of higher quality. That reductionist view is plainly invalid. To me, quality is what makes this Prosecco fit for purpose, for me, right here, right now."

"But you've just said that you prefer bubbles from the New World," counters Steph.

"Of course I'd like to be holding a glass of sparkling Chardonnay from Napa, close to my birthplace, but there aren't any on the wine list and I don't feel like going to a posh wine bar just to get one. That's the thing with quality: it connects us with the Cactus Bleu experience. The delicious cocos, the amiable staff and a cool atmosphere are all part of it. As for the wine, this Prosecco does the job: it delivers the functional and emotional benefits I expect from a glass of bubbles."

"Which are?"

"A legal high and a hint of celebration. I wouldn't mind having a taste of California on top of that, as I said, but I can do without it. A Prosecco does just fine."

"But you'd feel better still if you had a wider choice of sparkling wines on the list?"

"Sure, we're always better off with a choice," answers Maggie. "Imagine if this place were restricted to women, would you be happy?"

The biker has taken off his helmet, revealing a most attractive face. He sits down at the empty table.

"No," says Steph.

"Sorry, I thought this table was free," says the elegant biker and gets up again.

"No … I mean, yes … well I was just saying no to *her*, not to you…" Steph stutters.

Maggie can't believe her luck: Steph is handing him to her on a plate. She comes swiftly to the rescue.

"Please stay! You're most welcome. We were talking about free trade, choices and quality, so she's a bit confused. But don't worry: the table is free … and so are we."

She's amazed she's had the guts to say that to a complete stranger. She looks down and blushes.

"Thrilling debate, it seems… And you say I'm free to join in?" says the biker.

"Most definitely! This is Steph, the budding orator. I'm Maggie."

"Pleased to meet you. I'm Phaedrus."

III

"Let's have fun. Let's go shopping," says Maggie to Steph.

It's Monday and Steph's day off, as for most hairdressers. They drive to La Praille, the shopping centre. In the car, they start to reminisce about the nice evening they spent with Phaedrus, the drinks, the wit and the laughter; how handsome, refined and not the least bit intrusive he was; how they had decided to invite him for dinner next Saturday and how he had kindly accepted their offer to cook him a nice simple meal. Now they'll have to show that they're up to it.

Today, they are in the mood for a bit of shopping spree. The nice thing about La Praille is that it's got not just affordable clothes shops but also a bookshop, a movie theatre and a restaurant offering exotic foods. And there's a Coop hypermarket featuring a wide selection of wines. They pop in at various fashion shops, but they don't find anything worth spending money on and decide to see what wine they can buy for dinner with Phaedrus. He has told them that he likes to experiment with wines and that, like Maggie, he really enjoys drinking those from the New World.

They navigate the supermarket's aisles to the red wines section. Happily, the shelf tags sum up each wine in four brief lines: the first essentially gives the name of the brand or that of the producer; the following lines indicate its geographical origin (denoted with a neat little flag), the grape variety or varieties involved and, last but not least, a few suggestions for food pairing. Together with the price, this information should enable them to choose the right bottles for that evening. So far, they know they'll need a red wine because Steph will cook some pasta (that's what she does best).

"Should we also pick up a white wine or some bubbles for the apéritif?" Maggie enquires.

"Don't know," answers Steph, who keeps gazing at the huge wine wall.

"Well, we certainly can't afford to get the wines wrong, my dear, or he'll be utterly disappointed," says Maggie, who starts to feel a bit dazed in front of all those bits of information. Earlier, in the clothes shops, they were bombarded with music and various other "marketing primes". She now feels a bit exhausted and demotivated, and slips into what neuromarketers call a "mystery mood": she's getting confused and also senses her willpower declining. She can't take the risk of buying *any* wine from the New World. Nor can she just pick two pricey bottles that look good or have an appealing name but might not taste good or match the dish Steph intends to cook. She really wants to surprise Phaedrus with good wines, i.e. with quality.

"Steph, I've got to get out of here. Let's have a drink in a café and decide what to do next," she says.

Twenty minutes and a hot chocolate later, she feels that her motivation to buy the right wines for the dinner with Phaedrus has come back, strengthened. Henceforth, she'll pursue her goal unrelentingly. She's also determined to reduce the risk of getting the wrong wines and she's willing to pay a premium for that.

"We've got wheels and it's not rush hour yet, so let's drive to the Mövenpick store in Meyrin," says Maggie resolutely. "Coop sells very decent wines at quite affordable prices. It's a sort of guarantee of quality, just like that offered by a good brand, but we're not choosing a wine for an ordinary occasion. Phaedrus is no ordinary man. At Mövenpick, the wine specialist, bottles are a bit more expensive but we can ask for help and even taste a few. I've never been disappointed with them. And it's quite a shopping experience too. You'll see, Steph, it's going to be fun!"

At Mövenpick the wines are neatly arranged on wooden shelves. It feels like being in a huge private cellar, almost like a library. There are prestigious names all around the walls, with what looks like very expensive wines in glass cabinets at the back of the shop. Right at the entrance, on the left, there are people gathered around two long tables with dozens of opened bottles, glasses and a few snacks.

Maggie smiles back at the girls at the counter and grabs two glasses. She hands one to Steph.

"Hey," says Steph, "can we really taste all those bottles?"

"Sure, that's what the wines are here for. Don't worry, the girls won't bother us. They're knowledgeable, friendly and not pushy at all. It's their technique: they want you to feel comfortable so you while away a bit of time, you buy one item, then two… and then a few more bottles. That's the way it works. You just need to be very careful!"

"You mean, they just want us to discover and buy new wines? Can't complain about that!" says Steph.

"Well, they just happen to know that however naturally curious and drawn to novelty we may be, in the end we'll only trust what's familiar."

"Proposing something new that feels familiar! That's the holy grail of marketing. Right?"

"Yeah, sort of. One of the nice things about wine is that a lot of it is about discovery," says Maggie. "Still, that can be a problem, because often there's no way of figuring out what a wine will really taste like on the basis of the information that's given to us."

"What about those stories of the 'taste of terroir'? And hasn't each grape variety got its own taste?"

"True," says Maggie, "some studies have shown that a wine's taste can be largely reduced to the grape variety featured on the label. A few other cues might help in assessing it: medals, Parker's points and other types of recommendations in the wine literature, by friends, or by the staff here. There's no substitute for tasting the wine ourselves however, because that reduces a lot the risk associated with buying a new wine by making it familiar to us, and that's exactly what these people are doing here."

"Sounds cool."

"Yes, but watch out! Here, store and staff are brain-friendly. They don't just make it easy to find and choose what you want, they'll also make it easy to pay and, worse, you'll be tempted to trade up all the while. So you'd better be on high alert, because everything looks nice and attractive around here."

Maggie's normal shopping style is characterised by a combination of promotion-orientation (she likes unbeatable offers) and a relatively high level of pain – so much so that she's even got a reservation price of about 20 francs for a bottle of wine, which she usually refuses to exceed. But today is different: she's come here on a luxury shopping trip, to get quality and novelty in an attempt to impress Phaedrus. She knows that this is a dangerous place, and sets herself consciously in "prevention-orientation" mode: she wants strong guarantees that the wines she chooses "have quality" (as Pirsig would say). And since she isn't too confident about her own ability to assess quality through tasting alone, she's going to ask for help.

There are some Spanish bubbles for tasting, but the bottle is kept in the fridge, so they ask the girls if they can take it out and pour themselves some.

"Sure, go ahead," comes the reply from the desk, "and if you need assistance, just let us know."

It's a cava. Affordable, but Maggie and Steph find it a bit acidic. They also want something a bit more fruity.

They know that a pricey Champagne would be a safe choice, but that would likely be well over budget.

"What about a sparkling Chardonnay from Argentina or the US?" the manager asks.

She recommends a bottle from the state of Washington.

"Come on, I'll open the bottle for you," she says.

They like it, and have a friendly chat. Maggie wonders whether they have sparkling Shiraz. She has such fond memories of drinking those bubbles with the chicken tikka dishes she'd buy from nearby Marks & Sparks when she lived in Craig's New Town in the centre of Edinburgh. She turns to Steph.

"Any chance you're going to cook some chicken?"

"No. Just spicy pasta."

They spot an open bottle of "normal" Shiraz on the tasting table, amongst Cabernets from California, Malbecs from Argentina, and an array of Bordeaux, Chiantis, Riojas and a few red wines from the Valais and Geneva. They pour themselves a glass.

"See, I love the deep colour and you can really taste the grape," says Maggie to a pleasantly surprised Steph.

"What about a Pinot Noir from the Valais?" says Steph.

"OK, fine, let's have a drop, but only in your glass, so we can really compare the wines."

It is really good but a bit pale and lighter in comparison with the Shiraz. They don't think they could impress Phaedrus with it. They move on. Steph grabs a red blend from Geneva.

"Shall we try this one, Maggie?"

"It's quite good, and handcrafted by a woman," says a deep, authoritative voice standing next to them. "She's an innovative winemaker," he continues. "I usually drive to her winery nearby and buy directly from her." The man pauses for a second and stares at them over his circular glasses before continuing. "But really, you should go for this Bordeaux. It's quite impressive. Every drop is worth its high price."

Maggie and Steph giggle. This man is a real Swiss *traditionaliste*, knowledgeable and wealthy. Drinking wine is a pleasure to him and must reflect his social status, and Maggie knows that a high price is his main criterion for choosing a bottle, way ahead of its origin. *Traditionalistes* seek information from specialists and magazines about the wines prior to purchasing them. They are a bit like hunters intent on making a rational choice. They buy mostly from specialists and directly from producers. French wines have an excellent reputation in their eyes. *Traditionalistes* are not a rare species; quite the opposite. Maggie remembers reading that they're called "classic connoisseurs" in Britain, largely because they have a sound knowledge of the product and closely identify with Old World styles, but you might still catch them sipping wines from Australia or Chile.

The man acknowledges that some Australians can produce excellent wines (there's a 600 franc bottle in the glass cabinet near the counter), but he tries hard to win Maggie and Steph over to his cause. As he whirls his wine ostentatiously in his glass, he uses carefully chosen words like "perfect balance", "complexity" and "heritage" to describe it. In vain: they just keep giggling like two schoolgirls. They decide to move along and try a few other reds, have a snack, and go back to the first table to taste a few more bubbles. Save for the presence of that lone "connoisseur", the atmosphere is pretty relaxed around the tables. They eventually proceed to the checkout.

The girl at the counter confirms that the Shiraz is an excellent choice that won't let them down, but she encourages them to take a bottle of blanc de blancs, i.e. an all-Chardonnay Champagne, as a back-up, "just in case".

"There's a superb one that happens to be 40% off at the moment," she says. "It's a sure bet. Guaranteed. You know, for some people it *has* to be Champagne. They can be prickly."

"OK," says Maggie.

The credit card slides effortlessly into the reader. Maggie glances at the total. It hurts, yes, but not as much as she'd anticipated, for she immediately starts to rationalise the purchase, reminding herself that, after all, she's on a luxury shopping trip and it's all for a good cause. The bottles are handed to them with elegance and a graceful smile.

"That guy really took wine and himself seriously. What a pretentious bore!" says Maggie as she slips into the car. "And he's not even half as elegant or refined as our Phaedrus."

"He's certainly not as cool," adds Steph.

"Elegant cool," says Maggie. "Yes, that's what Phaedrus has."

They keep talking about him all the way home...

IV

Maggie sips her coffee whilst gazing at the snowflakes falling gently outside. They're so light that they seem to dance before landing on the balcony. "I really love this place," she tells herself, "and Phaedrus has wonderful taste."

"It looks like we won't be able to ski today," she says.

"You never know," says Phaedrus, smiling back at her. "It might clear up and we'd have nice powder. Conditions can change rapidly up here. And if it goes on snowing, I'll just write.

I'm a bit behind. Meanwhile, my muse could get her hair done." He gives her a loving gaze. "I've got a friend here, she's awfully nice and might even agree to fit you into her salon's busy schedule. Trust me, she really works wonders."

Well, Maggie thinks, Phaedrus certainly knows a thing or two about quality: his flat up here, his lifestyle – everything hints at quality. But how does one assess the quality of a hairdresser?

"What's a quality haircut?" she asks.

"Well, you can't define it just like that, not objectively. You have to experience it."

"C'mon, Phaedrus!"

"Yes. It's highly personal and it's dynamic."

"What?"

"Quality also comes as a sort of surprise. That's what Pirsig says in *Lila*."

"Yeah, yeah. Sure!"

"Well then, let me illustrate this with a neat little example."

"I'm all ears. Tell me."

"You know that ever since we met it's Steph who does my hair when I'm staying in Geneva."

"OK."

"About a month ago I needed a quick haircut, but she was off on holiday."

"So what's the point?"

"You also know that we like to stick to the familiar and don't really trust novelty, however alluring it may be?"

"Yeah, sure."

"Well, I went for Val."

"Val?"

"Yes, Steph's colleague. And guess what? She isn't just good-looking and charming, she really knows how to cut one's hair. Now that was a really nice surprise. It was quality through and through – an indefinably enjoyable experience!"

"Oh ha ha! And you're still chuffed about it!"

Maggie likes Phaedrus for his wit – and long blond hair. "It suits him almost as beautifully as it does that ravishing Calvin Klein model who used to grace all of the city's strategic points several years ago," she tells herself.

It is now snowing heavily outside. The flakes have grown smaller, but they are falling much more densely. It doesn't look as if it's going to stop any time soon. "What is quality snow?" she asks herself. Maggie has studied philosophy and knows all about problems of definition. She decides to challenge Phaedrus to define quality.

"What does the dictionary say about quality?" she enquires with a smile.

A good sport, he gets up and grabs the *Oxford Concise*.

"It says it's 'general excellence'."

"See? What you were saying earlier is that your nice friend up here – and that Val – are generally excellent at cutting hair. Simple." Maggie giggles.

"No. I was merely stating that I *perceive* that they deliver an excellent service. Quality, like value, is a perceptual experience that can't be defined in general terms. We can only talk about *perceived* quality or value, and these are very personal experiences. You have to experience them yourself."

"So it's a bit like wine" she says. "The quality of haircuts and wines is almost impossible to evaluate prior to experiencing them, right?"

"Exactly, that's why we have to rely on certain attributes like the good looks of the salon or bottle. But our own perception of quality, and of the attributes and cues signalling it, changes over the years, along with our expectations and tastes. So our relationship with quality isn't static. It's quite dynamic."

"You mean that we change – just like the world around us," says Maggie, adding: "Isn't Pirsig saying something in the same vein when he claims that quality itself changes, that it's dynamic at first but then eventually – and almost irremediably – becomes static in the end?"

"Yes, and you may remember that he uses a nice metaphor – that of a catchy tune that you hear by chance. It comes to you as a wonderful surprise. You track the record down, purchase it, but eventually discard it because you've got tired of listening to it over and over again: its quality has gone from dynamic to static in spite of the song remaining the same."

"I do," says Maggie. A negative definition occurs to her – always a handy way of getting round a problem – and she adds: "So we could say that, except for stuffy *traditionalistes*, quality is not the same as high prices or luxury and therefore it must be found at every price level."

"All right," says Phaedrus.

"And we can also say that, since it's never static but dynamic, quality requires continuous improvement – a little bit of *kaizen*, in other words."

Phaedrus can't help smiling. "She's really dynamic herself," he thinks.

"Yep," he says. "I have just read that some oenologists claim there are two concurrent definitions of wine quality. One, negative, is the absence of flaws in aroma or flavour. The other, positive, is the nearness to a target wine style. The latter involves taking into account not just winemakers' views, but wine consumers' sensory abilities, experience, expectations and personal preferences. In California, they're confident that consumer profiling is moving from art to science."

"OK, I suppose we can trust the Americans when they claim that they have made huge progress in matters of individual profiling over the past decade or so, but it stills looks like a long shot, and a bit complicated too. So couldn't we just say that a quality wine or a quality haircut is one that's 'fit for purpose'?" enquires Maggie, adding without pause: "It looks like it's going to snow for a while. I don't want to stand in the way of your work, and since you seem to recommend your friend's salon, I think I'll take you up on your offer. I'm in the mood for it. Could you possibly book her now and walk me there later on?"

"With pleasure. I love to walk in the snow. It's so wonderfully silent!" says Phaedrus. He picks up his mobile, has a brief but warm conversation with his friend and switches it off.

"She's ever so accommodating!" he says. "Her place is a hive of activity at the moment but she agrees to take you at 6:30. She keeps surprising me."

"That's because she has quality," chuckles Maggie.

"Where were we?" asks Phaedrus.

"We were wondering whether in the end quality simply means fitness for purpose."

"The answer is: yes, to a large extent. It's now clear that when we're about to purchase a wine offered to us at a certain price, we swiftly and mostly unconsciously consider the various benefits we expect from it for the occasion or mood we have in mind. To do our quick evaluation, however, we usually rely only on a few salient attributes and cues hinting at the benefits we seek. We also take several other shortcuts in order to make our choice. And when we fail to see the bottle of wine we're looking for, we might just grab a similar one and decide that it'll do the job, because we perceive it as having roughly the same quality or value as the one we were thinking of originally."

"But now you seem to talk about quality and value indiscriminately, just like Pirsig does," says Maggie.

"Well, he goes further and argues that quality, value and truth are all the same."

"If that's the case, then quality and value necessarily imply authenticity, and that can't be bad for us consumers, can it?"

"You're probably right. But to answer your earlier remark, we need to appreciate that quality and value are closely related. They are blurred and highly subjective constructs that only exist in someone's mind. The *perceived* quality or value of a wine or hair salon is a very personal affair – the result of emotional tagging. They are both charged with lots of emotional markers."

"You mean *somatic* markers – those non-conscious feelings formed by previous physical experience?"

"Yes, it's the same thing. We're instinctively drawn to or repelled by these markers, so they serve as an emotional guide and allow us to decide extremely rapidly by offering us non-conscious shortcuts right through our deliberations. But they can greatly influence our final appraisal of an offer."

"Then a very good gauge for the perceived value of a wine must be our willingness – or refusal – to pay a certain price for it."

"Well, sometimes we are willing to pay a bit more than anticipated, in order to reduce risk or for the sake of more convenience. But you're right: in neuromarketing terms, an excessive price is just a repulsive attribute that can play a decisive role in the simple process that the act of buying turns out to be."

"Is choosing – or buying – really such a simple process, and might 'simplified' not be a better word for it?" retorts Maggie. "Some people noticed in the late Seventies that when we evaluate an offer and eventually decide to purchase the product, there's a good dose of mindlessness on our part. So we've known for quite some time that we're pretty lazy decision-makers!"

"That's right. But what's new is that we're not that lousy after all, and that our choices, however suboptimal, are rarely inappropriate because, instead of examining every aspect of an offer, we somehow decide to rely on taking those shortcuts that make our lives so much simpler."

"Like what?"

"When we are faced with complex information, for instance, we often use only the most salient information at our disposal. You must have experienced that a thousand times! Another shortcut is that we usually take what is first presented to us as the reference point. It's called 'anchoring': 'It's 18 carat gold and is worth 18,000 francs,' I was told a few months ago by a shop assistant attempting to sell me a 1,399 franc gold-coloured laptop that immediately felt much less expensive, almost like a bargain. Retailers are known to display more expensive products alongside those they most want us to buy."

"That's a bit naughty," says Maggie.

"Yes. Well, I didn't fall for that one – it was a bit too obvious – but that particular trick is widely used in retailing. The fact that we react differently depending on how an attribute is presented to us is called 'attribute framing'. That also affects our final appraisal. Identifying the most critical wine attributes and knowing how (i.e. in which frame) to present them to us, is vital for marketers attempting to influence our choice, because a single attribute will sell a product when the information about it is put in the right context."

"But that's what in psychology we call the 'framing effect'," says Maggie: "the fact that we react to a particular choice in different ways depending on how it's presented to us, especially when it's formulated in terms of a gain or a loss. So what you're saying is that context matters more than content. This implies that the environment in which the valuation is done is important too. The type of store or restaurant we're in when we select a wine, for instance, and whether we're alone or surrounded by people who might be watching us: all these situational factors must impact on our final choice. Right?"

"Yes, and all this means that our evaluation of a wine or hair salon is likely to be biased in the end. Our choice is suboptimal since it's the outcome of a decision process that actually bypasses the rational (deliberative and analysing) stage it's supposed to go through. To sum it up: we consumers are somewhat irrational, quite emotional and, since we keep taking the same shortcuts, we're very predictable too."

"The problem is, my dear, that I like to think of myself as being rather unpredictable!" Maggie retorts.

"What makes you so sure that you aren't predictable to neuromarketers and how do you propose to do defeat their cunning plans anyway?"

"With quality," says Maggie. "With what Pirsig calls this 'sense of betterness' that is ingrained in Native American culture and that turns you into a bit of a rebel eventually. Because the only predictable thing about rebels is that they won't let others manipulate them easily. What you'd also need is greater awareness and more education, because when you know your adversaries' language, you're so much better equipped to outwit their schemes. For instance, knowing that marketers can't make you buy something you really don't want, that they can't press a magic 'buy button' in you, can be quite a helpful thought. And then, call it luck or providence, there's always a chance that even the best plans to manipulate other people's thoughts might go awry. Got a neat example for you."

"OK. Shoot!"

"In California, my father once found himself sitting at a café table next to a Hoopa chief, David Risling, who's now remembered as the 'father of Indian education'. My dad told him that when he was a kid he used to watch a weekly American children's program – a western – on Swiss television but that his sympathy kept falling on the Indian side. The chief smiled, then gently grasped his arm and said these productions were just Hollywood propaganda aimed at young white Americans. It was meant to portray the American natives as savages, so white kids could feel better about their forebears decimating the Indians and ripping the land from them. He was genuinely pleased to see that white men's spin had got out of control and backfired on them."

Phaedrus gets up, puts some gentle music on and comes back to her with open arms.

"Fancy a White Deer Skin Dance, my dear?" he asks, chuckling.

"Oh, got you. Fine!"

V

Maggie and Phaedrus top a wonderful day of skiing with a few drinks at the Paragon bar that stands right at the bottom of the slopes. Later, they decide to have luxury bubbles and some food inside. Maggie picks up the sleek black menu.

"There's only one white, one red and one rosé to choose from their 'wine corner', and the 'bubbles all over' section offers just one Champagne! And look at the prices!" Maggie gasps.

"Well, that's Verb. It comes with fancy price tags. Everything's a bit extreme here," says Phaedrus.

"Oh, there are some gambas. That looks tasty, but they're almost twice as expensive as the cocos we usually eat at the Cactus Bleu," she says.

They both order gambas and a glass of Champagne.

"Marketers know that we're lazy decision-makers," says Phaedrus, "so we'd better set our brains on high alert whenever we walk into a high price zone like this, or we'll end up consuming the high prices more than the food or the wines."

"You mean that these bubbles and these shrimps might taste better just because they're more expensive?" says Maggie.

"Yes, whenever we're aware of the price of a wine, we might no longer be capable of enjoying it solely on the merits of its organoleptic qualities. It's been shown that a higher price results in a better evaluation of the same wine. The area of the brain that seems to be affected is the one that integrates purely organoleptic information with expectations about the taste of the wine based on information about its price or its brand name."

"That's stunning."

"Indeed, and roughly the same happens with locally grown food products, which people find tastier, healthier and of higher quality than the same product offered under a national label."

"Now I understand why Steph prefers to drink local wines. How does that work?"

"Neuromarketers call it the 'placebo effect of brand expectations'. When you deal with strong brands or strong appellations, people may actually be consuming the *expectations* more than the wine itself."

"Wow! You mean, it's the experience that's shaped by the brand, and not the opposite!" says Maggie. "That's why strong brands are so powerful, and that must be why they can usually command a higher price."

"Shaping expectations that are strong enough to influence a consumption experience is only one of the key functions of a brand name," Phaedrus says. "Another important role is to provide shortcuts when alternatives are difficult to evaluate."

"Like when I'm lost in front of my supermarket's wine wall? But aren't brands, like appellations, meant to provide assurance of consistency and quality? That's a rather useful role in such a volatile and confusing world. There's so much variability in quality and price! Tell me how we can best reduce the risk of making an unsatisfactory choice," says Maggie.

"Choosing a well-known appellation or brand name and paying the premium for it is a natural response on our part and a common way of reducing that kind of risk. Another solution is to walk to a specialist's shop. Call it convenience or something else, it just means that, unlike 'classic connoisseurs' (or *traditionalistes*), we're not ready to invest the time and effort necessary to seek the relevant information about the wines offered in shops."

"You've got to be pretty hooked to do that!"

"Specialists are here to provide tasting and advice," Phaedrus says. "That's where *internationalistes* usually go. Their profile's a bit like that of *traditionalistes*, though to them it's not the price but the country of origin that's the most important attribute for choosing a wine: French and Spanish wines enjoy an excellent image with them. Most *internationalistes* are over sixty, male, well educated and wealthy. It feels as though there are quite a few of them in this café."

The way Phaedrus expresses it betrays the fact that he doesn't quite belong to this crowd, and Maggie senses it all too clearly: "He is younger, cooler and far more enlightened than the loud people surrounding us," she thinks.

"Let's get out of here," says Maggie.

It's pretty cold outside. The sky is clear and Orion twinkles above the white mountain tops that can be made out in the dark. Because they've had a bit of luxury already, they think twice about having a top-notch dining or clubbing experience and decide to spend the evening at home. They pick up a pizza on the way and pass in front of a few well-lit luxury wine shops. Once they've got back to the flat, Phaedrus has a surprise for Maggie: a few bottles of sparkling Shiraz from the state of Victoria, down under, and a wonderful sparkling Chardonnay from California.

"I bought these bottles on my last trip to London," he says. "I knew you liked that style of wine. They're not that expensive, but they're relatively hard to come by in this country."

"What an exclusive treat. That's true luxury," says Maggie.

They open one of the bottles of sparkling Shiraz whilst eating the pizza. Maggie remains a little baffled by the fact that some people would actually want to "consume" or be seen to "consume" a famous name or a high price tag.

"Well," Phaedrus says, "wine can be used by aspirational consumers just like any other positional good, be it Chanel skis or Chloé après-ski gear."

"I can see what you mean by aspirational consumers – they aspire to a higher lifestyle or greater social recognition at the risk of looking like fools. But why talk about 'positional' goods? I presume it's because they're used by those people to position themselves, but where?"

"Amongst the rich. It can be any item as long as it's expensive. You've only got to look at this copy of *How to Spend It* to see some silly examples."

"Wow, look at this page!" Maggie squawks. "The model is wearing ski goggles that cost as much as the skis themselves!"

"Some of these items are extremely expensive only because the firms producing them won't sell them at a more affordable price."

"Or maybe they know how to starve the market!" she says.

"You're right, and likewise for wine: some of the priciest bottles are only produced in limited quantities, when top quality grapes are available. The wines produced in less exceptional years are usually sold as sub-brands. Many top wine brands have strong ties with the luxury sector anyway. Chanel, for instance, which owns two châteaux in Bordeaux, has just acquired a winery in Napa Valley."

"A 50 franc glass of bubbly Chanel would suit the Paragon's wine list," Maggie jokes.

"Quite a few wine producers have adopted a 'Château Chanel' strategy and moved into that rarefied territory," says Phaedrus with a smile. "Luxury wine producers have sprouted everywhere from Napa to Mendoza."

"Even Calvinistic Geneva claims to have its own little icons!" she cuts in.

"Well, their success may also stem from consumers' search for more authentic (often meaning just 'more local') wines in an increasingly globalised world. Many of those customers are now millennials."

"But millennials are all digital. They're highly connected and much more sceptical and discerning than the older generation," Maggie says. "I've been told that millennials consuming luxury goods aren't showing them off in order to signal their status to others as much as their elders needed to do. The motivation of millennials is much more egoistic: they essentially want to please themselves. You've heard the line 'because I'm worth it'."

"Quite right," says Phaedrus. "Neuroscientists have spotted that luxury brands activate the area of the brain that deals with the perception of the 'self', which could hint at one's wish to transfer the status of the prestigious brand to one's 'self'."

"If millennials' preferences have shifted from 'outside' to 'inside', as I have heard, so must their sense of exclusivity," Maggie says. "Does this mean that exclusivity currently needs to reflect their personal system of values – that these consumers want to make a statement about how knowledgeable they are, or how they see the world?"

"Most definitely! And their message is aimed at like-minded people – at the crowd they want to belong to. They're interested in products that have a true story to tell, and in 'experiences'. Wine being essentially an experience good, that should bode well for winegrowers all around the world."

"But millennials are well-known for wanting something for their money," Maggie retorts. "Is this 'something' just 'something inessential, desirable, that is expensive or difficult to obtain', as your dictionary likes to define luxury?"

"I don't think so. Luxury may well still be about creating desire, but just offering a high price and some degree of rarity won't do the trick any more. You need products that are both appealing and convincing in terms of how and where they're produced, plus you need a good story that customers with limited attention span will buy into. Still, to underpin its legitimacy, luxury needs quality."

To emphasise the point, Phaedrus pushes towards her a small envelope that has been lying around for several days, alongside the bottles of sparkling wine.

"A little luxury experience for you," he says.
Inside there is a ticket for a day of heli-skiing.
"You're spoiling me, my love!"

Three days later, optimal conditions are finally met for a day of heli-skiing. Maggie, a guide and two other experienced skiers board a helicopter bound for the Petit Combin in search of some good deep snow. Soon afterwards, the guide spots a nice thick cornice that looks like a possible touchdown area. The pilot decides to test its strength with the skid. It resists the pressure well, and clearance is given to alight from the hovering aircraft. The rotor's downwash produces a constant flurry of snow, so the skiers must bend to protect their faces whilst the guide swiftly unloads all their skis and poles. Seconds later, the pilot is given the thumbs-up. The helicopter rises gently whilst gracefully turning on itself and dives down into the valley.

This is the nearest to a perfect day that one could possibly get. A lot of snow has fallen in the previous days, but the sky is bright blue at present. It's cold too, so the powder is extremely light – so light, in fact, that it splashes onto Maggie's face with every turn she makes. She's glad she took her big goggles and a scarf to protect her mouth so that she can breathe in properly. At one point, just before cresting a little ridge, she lets the other skiers go. They move out of her sight for a precious moment, which she uses to get this incredible feeling of oneness with her magnificent surroundings. Not a single sound, just that of a light breeze caressing the surface of the snow. After three minutes or so she pursues her descent. The rest of the party has stopped about half a mile below, anxiously wondering what has happened to her. She waves to them to signal that everything is fine.

Maggie spots a nice corridor, full of immaculate snow, a hundred meters further to the right of their tracks. She decides to "put her signature" there and crosses the slope to reach it. She makes a dozen elegant, beautifully cadenced turns. Then, suddenly, she feels as if the entire slope is moving down the mountainside, at ever greater speed. She tries to control her skis, but the lateral pressure is much too strong. She falls. Everything goes white. Everything seems to slide down with her.

"Gosh, it's an avalanche," she tells herself. "I must keep on top of it."

Freja's words spring to her mind: "Just float, take it easy, float through life."

POSTFACE

The four profiles of Swiss wine drinkers *(indifférents, curieux, traditionalistes and internationalistes)* that are referred to in our story are portrayed in:

- Ferjani, Ali, Mann, Stefan, Reissig, Linda et Ayala, Tatiana (2010) 'Préférences des consommateurs de vin en Suisse', *Revue suisse Viticulture, Arboriculture, Horticulture*; Vol 42(5), pp 278–284.

The 'Chardonnay girl' is one of the six profiles drawn by Waverley. Her full portrait and that of the other five types of UK wine drinkers (the easily pleased, the entertainer, the enthusiast, the adventurer and the classic connoisseur) are featured in:

- Waverley (2003) 'Wine at face value', in *Wine List 2003/04*, Waverley TBS, Hemel Hempstead.

A wine's main attributes are its colour, origin, varietal character and winemaking style, alcoholic strength, packaging, brand name and price. You can read more about them in:

- Spahni, Pierre (1995, 2000) *The International Wine Trade*, Woodhead Publishing, Abington/Cambridge.
- ----------------- et Labys, Walter C. (1992) *Le Vin*, Economica (Cyclope), Paris.

The links between attributes and the perceived quality and value of beverages run through the benefits suggested by those attributes and by other cues, but our perception of these attributes and cues changes over time, as do our tastes and expectations. Quality and value are only mental constructs. You'll find more on this (and haircuts) in:

- Zeithalm, Valarie A. (1988) 'Consumer Perceptions of Price, Quality, and Value: A Means-End Model and Synthesis of Evidence', *Journal of Marketing*, July 1988; Vol 52, pp 2–22.

Pirsig's philosophical approach to quality and value is laid out in two novels, though principally in his later work *Lila*:

- Pirsig, Robert M. (1974) *Zen and the Art of Motorcycle Maintenance – An Inquiry into Values.* William Morrow and Company, Inc., New York.
- -------------------- (1991) *Lila – An Inquiry into Morals.* Bantam Books, New York.

Trust, beliefs and taste; quality and our incapacity to assess it on an objective basis;

our rationalising about what we have already decided subconsciously – all these issues are dealt with in the following work on applied psychology:

- von Holzschuher, Ludwig (1955) *Praktische Psychologie – Die Primitivperson im Menschen* (2. Auflage), Heering Verlag, Seebruck am Chiemsee.

The fundamentals of neuromarketing that have been used throughout our story are laid out in:

- Genko, Stephen J., Pohlmann, Andrew P. and Steidl, Peter (2013) *Neuromarketing for Dummies*, John Wiley Canada, Mississauga.

The relationship between price and perceived quality (and why we can't assess a wine purely on its organoleptic properties when we know its price in particular), plus the impact that luxury brands have on the self, are taken from:

- Roullet, Bernard et Droulers, Olivier (2010) *Neuromarketing – Le marketing revisité par les neurosciences du consommateur.* Dunod, Paris.

On 'attribute framing' and on why taking those shortcuts that make our life so much simpler may not be so irrational after all, read:

- Oxera (2013) *Behavioural Economics and its Impact on Competition Policy,* Oxera Consulting, Oxford.

Quality and luxury are dealt with in various issues of the *Handelszeitung* and of the *Financial Times,* as well as in a special report on luxury ('Exclusively for Everybody') issued by *The Economist* on December 13th 2014.

An historical perspective on the Swiss wine market's relationship with quality can be gained from:

- Schellenberg, Alfred (1937) 'Schweizerische Weinwirtschaft in den Jahren 1885–1936', in

Forschungen auf dem Gebiete der Wirtschaftswissenschaften des Landbaues (Festgabe Ernst Laur), pp 467–484. Brugg, Effingerhof.

- Dubois, Jacques (1944) *Le vigneron vaudois et ses vins (comment il pourra en améliorer la vente)*. Thèse, Lausanne, Imp. Centrale.

Evidence for the argument that the perceived taste of a wine can be largely reduced to the grape variety featured on the bottle's label, can be found in:

- Corduas, Marcella, Cinquanta, Luciano and Ievoli, Corrado (2013) 'The importance of wine attributes for purchase decisions: A study of Italian consumers' perception', *Food Quality and Preference* 28, pp 407–418.

The finding that locally produced wines are perceived as having higher quality – mostly on the grounds that buying them boosts people's cultural identity – is provided in:

- Barena Figueroa, Ramo and Sanchez Garcia, Mercedes (2007) 'Connecting Product Attributes with Emotional Benefits. Analysis of a Mediterranean Product across Consumer Age Segments', Mediterranean Conference of Agro-Food Social Scientists, EAAE Seminar on *Adding Value to the Agro-Food Supply Chain in the Future Euromediterranean Space*, Barcelona, April 23rd–25th 2007.

Carolina Werle of the Grenoble Graduate School of Business was reported in the *Financial Times* of October 12th 2015 as having uncovered evidence that people find locally grown food products tastier, healthier and of higher quality.

Linda Bisson of the University of California in Davis (as related in the April 2015 issue of *Wine Business Monthly*) is the oenologist offering the two concurrent definitions of wine quality.

ABOUT THE AUTHOR

Pierre Spahni comes from a family of wine brokers. Educated at the universities of Lausanne, California (Davis) and Newcastle upon Tyne, he holds doctorate degrees in Business Science and in Agricultural & Food Marketing. Now based in Geneva, he provides independent consultancy services to institutions and companies dealing with wine.

www.ingramcontent.com/pod-product-compliance
Lightning Source LLC
Chambersburg PA
CBHW071252170526
45165CB00003B/1315